The Art of The Text

The Ultimate Guide on Texting Girls

2nd Edition

By Zac Miller

Copyright © 2019
All Rights Reserved
ISBN: 9781983295393
Publisher: ZML Corp LLC

Table of Contents

Disclaimer

This book is written for informational and entertainment purposes only. This book is in no way affiliated with Facebook, Snapchat, or any other website or app.

This Page Intentionally Left Blank

Introduction

This book is the cumulative knowledge of what I have learned throughout my life in regards to texting girls. I have done hours and hours of research, talked with some of the top pick-up artists in the field, read every book I could get my hands on, and have made a guide that brings together the best aspects of all these. This is what got me the girls and what got me the responses. I put a lot of time and effort into this guide and hope you learn from it. Use the techniques laid out in this guide and you will succeed.

I go into great detail giving many example texts you can send, as well as the basic rules of texting, and proper text messaging techniques. I go over *everything* when it comes to texting a girl: how to get her number, the basics of good texting, the first message, many example situations, example text messages, texting her for a date, and what to do after the date. Enjoy!

P.S. You can find out more about me, as well as many informative articles on attracting women at my website GetMoreDates.com. I also have a section called "VIP Coaching" were you can sign up to receive personal coaching from me to help you in your journey of attracting women.

Chapter 1
Understanding Texting Now

———————————————

Within the last ten years, texting has really started becoming a vessel people rely on. Calls have become few and far between as it is much easier and non-invasive to just pick up your phone and send out a text. Then the recipient reads your text, and it's like any other conversation, except you get to think about your answer and can reply when you want to. And this is what is so big about texting; you get to reply with answers which you have time to think about.

Texting has also become a huge part of the dating world, as this is the first method of contact after getting a girl's phone number. Most girls expect a text first, and to call her first now-a-days almost seems rude and may turn a girl off if she doesn't know you that well. She is also much more likely to answer a text message, as opposed to a phone call which she will probably let go to voicemail, especially if she doesn't recognize the number.

This is why knowing how to text is such a big deal in today's society and can really make or break your chances with females. The thing about females is, unlike males, they are much more attracted to a partner's personality and character versus his looks alone. This means how you present yourself is a very important factor. Now you may be a nice, cool, fun guy... but just not very good at texting. So if your text messages make you seem boring, mean, or creepy, there is a good chance she will stop responding and leave you out to dry. Unfortunately she doesn't have much else to judge you by as text messages may be the only means of contact you have kept with her. For this reason, she may never find out your true personality, which she may have been very attracted to.

When you're texting a girl you want to build an image of yourself as a fun, flirtatious guy who she is going to want hang out with and get to know more. Then you need to understand that the main purpose of texting is to either set up a phone call to talk with a girl, or to set up a date with a girl. This is because you build rapport and comfort with girls when you talk to them on the phone and when you are physically with them on dates. Building attraction with a girl comes from physical, face to face interaction and phone calls; texting can only do so much.

There's an equation that you must remember for you to have your best chance of girls accepting your date, as well as not flaking on you. The equation goes like this:

Goal of texting = Building rapport
Building rapport = Getting her to agree to a date
Getting her to agree to a date = ATTRACTION

You see it's the actual face to face interaction with a girl that will build attraction between the two of you and get her to become interested in you; texting is just a stepping stone to get there. This is why I preach in my book to text fun, witty, sarcastic text messages to girls and to be unpredictable, but I make sure to emphasize that you DO NOT text her forever! You lose so much mystery and attraction this girl may have had for you when you text her too much. Not only that:

- *You can bore her*
- *She could take something you say over text the wrong way*
- *It can get annoying to be texted too much from one guy*

So yes, texting can make or break how a girl views you, but remember it is not the only tool to use in your arsenal of attracting a female.

You see what happens when you text a female too much is the conversation ends up getting stale. You can only say what's up, lol, and haha so many times.

When you try to force conversations, it has bad outcomes. You end up becoming just another guy texting her. That's something else you have to acknowledge about girls... especially very attractive girls... you are NOT the only guy texting her. She is getting texts from multiple guys. So in essence, you are competing with them, and the one who attracts her the most via text is going to win.

Chapter 2
The Foundation

There are three items which are the foundation of my texting strategy. Most guys don't do any of these, which is why they fail when texting women. What are these three items I speak of?

- Be Fun
- Be Unpredictable
- Be a Challenge

Be Fun

There's a song by Cyndi Lauper called "Girls Just Want to Have Fun." You should go listen to it if you haven't heard it. This is an important rule when texting girls. Girls do NOT want boring, mundane, recycled texts on their phone. Are you guilty of any of the following:

- Whats up?

- What you doing?
- How was your day?
- Hey beautiful
- Hey

Girls just want to have fun... what does that mean? It means girls want a fun, challenging, intelligent guy who doesn't give into their every wish and doesn't send them boring texts like the ones above. If I can give you one rule to remember when texting, this is it, girls just want to have fun. So during your texts tease her, make fun of her, take things out of context, use ambiguity, double entendre, and have fun with your text messages! Girls just want to have fun! This will not only make *you* look fun, but will also make you appear unique from the other guys who are texting her messages like "how was your day" and other boring texts. These are lame, boring texts which do not build any emotional attraction with girls. If this girl doesn't know you that well, what's provoking her to talk with you? What's making her say "I want to text this guy back"? I provide a more extensive list of examples in Chapter 5, but let's look at a better first text you could send her.

"I'm bored, let's rob a bank. Do you want to be the getaway driver or the robber?"

What other guy has ever sent her anything like this? When she picks up her phone and sees this text, what is she going to think of you? She's going to think you're a fun guy who she wants to talk to.

Now I'm not saying you have to come up with the most outlandish, creative opening for all of your texts. Sometimes your mind goes blank and you can't think of anything, and not all girls take the same humor. But be original. Instead of saying "hi" say something like "hola amiga". Be fun!

Be Unpredictable

One of the goals of texting a girl is to get her interested in you and continuing to think about you even when you're not around. When you are predictable, girls get bored. When you text her back as soon as she texts you, when you text her at the same time every morning, when you text her every day, you are predictable. Predictability is a sin when it comes to texting; it kills your chances with girls.

By being unpredictable, girls will not be able to "figure you out"; this builds tension, as well as attraction with women. When a girl doesn't know when you will text her, what you will text her or if you will text her, it leaves her on her toes and thinking about you all day.

So what do I mean by be unpredictable? Respond quickly to one of her texts, but then wait an hour before you respond to another. Text her at night one day, then text her in the morning another. Have different openers when you text her. Be unpredictable!

Here's a technique to use once in a while to be unpredictable. Let's say you're having an exciting text conversation with a girl and the texts are going back and forth pretty quickly. The next time she texts you don't respond and drop off for a little while. You know how this feels when girls do it to you, so flip it on her! She's going to get uncertain and wonder things like:

- "Why isn't he texting me back?"
- "Did I do something wrong?"
- "Should I have sent that text?"
- And the many more things girls may think to themselves

Also, this makes her want you more. Girls want what they can't have! So when you do text her back like 20 minutes later, or an hour later, or however long you wait, she'll feel that sense of relief and get butterflies from the adrenaline rush your text delivers. She'll only feel that kind of pleasure after she has had a feeling of loss. By being unpredictable you'll be golden!

So text her back right away, text her back in 10 minutes, text her back in 10 hours. Sometimes I even wait till the next day. You just don't want to look like you are sitting by your phone waiting for her text message, only to text her back the second she hits "send." This makes you look desperate. Not only that, you want a girl to experience a wide range of emotions to keep her interested in you. By changing up your response time you create suspense which will hit her emotional buttons. (Being unpredictability ties into challenge, which I talk about next).

Be a Challenge

Girls want what they can't have; it is reverse psychology at its finest. When you are always available, always responding, and always texting her first, girls will lose interest in you fast. Being too available is not a good thing; there's no chase for the girl, there's no **challenge**.

I noticed something peculiar after getting girl's numbers and chasing them for dates... the girls I seemed more into, as in the ones I put more effort into and tried to always text and call them, ended up being less likely to return my phone calls and texts. But then the ones I kind of blew off and didn't show much interest in wouldn't stop trying to contact me. How bizarre? This doesn't make sense? It all makes sense when you think about challenge though.

So what exactly do I mean by "be a challenge?" Think about how girls treat you. They may text you back one word answers, wait hours before they text you back, not text you back at all, etc. I want you to use this thinking, and turn it around on them. Being a challenge is one of the best tactics you can use when you are trying to attract a female. Remember, girls want what they cannot have. So when you're a challenge and she can't have you, she will want you!

So because of this "rarity" and "want what they can't have" factor girls seem to love, I have incorporated advice on adapting it to texting. Here are some guidelines:

Be Concise. Shorter texts get far more replies than longwinded ones.

Stay Positive. No one likes a downer; bring positive energy to your texts. Girls should look forward to receiving texts from you. Let them dread texts from those other boring, depressing, life-draining guys, while you come along and light up their days.

Keep It to a Few Texts. Unless you get into a really good texting conversation with a girl you'll want to keep it to generally just a few texts.

I incorporate all three of my foundation topics, being fun, being unpredictable, and being a challenge throughout the book. Come back to this section if you need help. These are the basis of my texting strategy.

Chapter 3
Getting Her Number

The first thing you need in order to text a girl is her phone number. Some of you may have this step down already, but I did not want to leave it out of the book as it is so important.

In Class or at Work

This is the easiest way to get a girls number, where the two of you share an atmosphere where you are familiar with each other and have already casually interacted. In a place like work or school, you really want to talk with the girl a little and have some interactions with her before you ask for her number. Cold openers can definitely work, and I will talk about them next, but you will have a better chance and it makes things a little easier if you have had previous interactions with a girl.

So let's say the two of you have a class together. Try and get a seat that's near her and interact with her during class. Make sure to introduce yourself and ask for her name (which I'm sure you already know) and talk about the homework, school gossip, anything really; you just want to make sure you are conversing with her and she knows who you are. If you sit across the class from her and then randomly ask for her number one day, you are much less likely to get it. In this type of situation, I have found asking for her number with a "purpose" is a good strategy.

What you need to remember is remain confident. You don't want her to see how nervous you are. If you have to write down the lines on a piece of paper and then rehearse them in front of your bathroom mirror, then do it. Just have a face of confidence when you talk to her, as it makes you look much more attractive.

So let's say you have been sitting near this girl, you have shared some conversations, and class is about to end. The first few days of class have gone by and you and this girl have talked a little. A great line to use is:

"Hey I don't really know many people in this class, could I get your number? Just in case I miss a class I'll have someone to ask what happened."

You could also go with:

"Nice meeting you Jessica. Could I get your number? I may need help with some of the work and you seem pretty smart."

In the above example, I gave a girl a compliment when I was asking for her number; I said she was smart. When giving girls compliments, do not compliment them on their looks, especially girls who are super attractive. They get this from guys all day. So when you comment on a piece of jewelry she's wearing, or some aspect of her personality, you stand out from other guys who are saying things like "you're hot". By giving her a compliment like this when asking for her number, it will make her feel good about herself and she will be more likely to provide it to you.

If you are at work, you're using a similar strategy. Talk to her, get to know her a little, converse with her. Then when you feel comfortable and are work acquaintances, you can ask for her number. A good work example would be:

"Hey Tiffany. I just realized I don't have your number. Could I get that from you?"

If you two know each other well, and you have talked awhile, there is a very high likelihood you will get her number in this situation. This line may seem very simple, and it is… but simple works. She will know what's going on, and if she likes you too, she will have no problem giving you her number. If she's not into you, you'll get some type of excuse from her. Just have to move on and work on yourself. You may need to let her go, or try again later in the future.

Out Somewhere

When you are out somewhere, I want to start off by saying you should ask for a girl's number as soon as possible. The reason being is the more time you wait and look at her, the more awkward the situation gets, the more anxiety that builds up, and the more of a chance she could leave before you get to say anything. Sometimes it's hard to muster up the courage, but the more you practice and the more girl's numbers you ask for, the easier it will get.

So you're out somewhere and just spotted a girl you want to start talking to. Do NOT use pick-up lines. They do not work, and unless you look like a model, you will most likely not get her number.

A great way to start a conversation is to make it seem like you have a purpose for talking to the girl. This works better than walking up to a girl and saying "let me get that number." Bring up something that she can start talking about and relate to. Examples would be if she is holding a new phone, you can go up to her and ask her about it because you're "thinking about getting one like it." If she has an interesting accessory on you can ask her where she got it from and how much it costs. If she goes to your high school or college, you can ask if she goes to your school. Even if you know she didn't go to your school or already know about the phone, it's okay, you're just using it as a talking point. Whatever answer you get, you should use to keep the conversation going. Here's an example:

Zac: Whoa, is that the new iPhone you have?

Girl: Yeah it is.

Zac: How do you like it? I'm thinking about getting one.

Girl: It's pretty sweet. I really like the camera.

If the girl is into you, she will most likely keep the conversation going. If she doesn't like you she will most likely give you a one word answer, or not give you a question back and walk away. You have to understand you can't get 100% of girls… but you can sure come close!

If she happens to walk away, don't think too much about it. There are billions of girls and just learn from your experiences. Sometimes it might not even be you! You could have said all the right things but she was just having a really bad day. You got to remember these things.

Now if she **IS** into you, she will most likely keep the conversation going and start asking you questions. So let's say the conversation continues:

Zac: *Oh that's great, the camera on my phone sucks, so I could use that. By the way, what's your name?*

Girl: *Sarah*

Zac: *Nice to meet you Sarah. Hey I got to run but I'd love to talk with you more another time. You think I could get your phone number?"*

Zac: *Okay it's 555-555-5555.*

This is really my go to line. It's simple, easy to remember, and gets the job done. You're telling her you're having a fun time and a good conversation, but have to run. You obviously want to keep talking to her, and the only way to do that is get her number. I have a high success rate with this line. It just works. Also, you always want to be the first to go. This includes text, phone, on the date, everything! This leaves her wanting more and missing you.

Let me give you an example of another line I used the other day. I had a very cute waitress who was taking care of me at a restaurant. When she brought out my drink there was no straw in it, however all my friends did have a straw. This was perfect. You're just looking for any little excuse you can use to talk to her. So after lunch was over, I ended up going up to her and telling her it was unacceptable I didn't get a straw in my drink, with a smile on my face. I told her I was going to tell her manager, and I needed her name and number. She immediately realized what was going on, laughed, and gave me her number. This is a great example of finding a purpose to ask for a girl's number.

Do NOT ask the girl on a date when you are talking to her. You have not build enough rapport with her and she will most likely decline. Just get her number and leave. You need to always take things slow with women. You should never ask her out on a date on the first text you send her either. You need to build rapport with a girl, which will increase your chances greatly of getting a date with her.

Another way to get a girl's number, which I actually use quite often, is to just be direct. Now this isn't for the faint of heart, and if you get nervous around girls this may be a little harder for you, but it is direct and gets right to the point. And each time you do it, it becomes easier and easier to do. Here is an example. In this example I will be in a grocery store:

> **Zac:** *Hey my name is Zac, I just saw you when I was walking by this aisle, and I think you're very attractive. You think I could get your phone number?*
>
> **Girl:** *Ummm okay.*
>
> **Zac:** *Thanks, I'll text you later (walk away).*

Yes, it really is that easy. You really don't need fancy lines or rehearsals to get a girl's phone number.

As long as you look presentable, have strong body language and appear confident while you are talking, you have a great chance of getting a number from this technique. Psychology teaches us that a person can tell if they are attracted to someone within seconds of meeting them. If she likes you, and is also attracted to you, she will give you her number. If she doesn't like you, she will most likely say something like "I have a boyfriend," or make up another excuse on why she can't give you her number. Don't take it personally, just work on yourself and move on. That's something else you need to understand, no one, not even Brad Pitt, can get every single girl. No man on this planet can do that. But with the right strategy, you can greatly increase your numbers.

Again, here is a chart I want to emphasize:

- Texting/Talking on Phone →
- Establishing Comfort and Rapport With a Girl →
- Successfully Getting Her to Agree and Not Flake on a Date With You

Getting a girl to feel comfortable with you is one of the best things you can do in order to guarantee a date with her.

Another tool you can use is Facebook. Facebook is wonderful for talking to girls! Let's say you know of a girl through friends, or there's a girl in school who is attractive but you've had no interaction with her, add her on Facebook. Most girls accept everyone's friend request. Use the tactics taught in this book on Facebook messenger, and transition into getting her number. Just know, Facebook adds another step to the process and makes things a little bit harder. So use this as a last resort if there is no way you are able to obtain a girl's phone number through other means.

As a token of appreciation to my readers, I am offering the report above titled *Subconscious Attraction: 3 Techniques That Will Attract Her Subconsciously* **absolutely free!** Just copy and paste the link below into your browser, put in your email address, and it will be immediately sent to you.

Linkpony.com/attract

Chapter 4
Texting Basics

It's not just *what* you text girls that will make you look attractive, but *how* you text them.

Conversation Speed

Let's start with conversation speed. By that I mean know when you are texting a girl too much or too fast. If you text a girl and she doesn't get back to you, wait a little bit; more than likely she is busy and will respond later. Sometimes I have girls respond hours later, or even the next day, to a text I have sent them. People have lives and may not be by their phone every second. If she is out getting her hair done and has eight text messages from you when she picks up her phone, you look desperate! This will immediately lower your chances of getting with this girl as it makes you look needy and clingy, two qualities that girls find unattractive. My general rule is a two text max. If she isn't texting you back and you think she has seen your message, you can send one more… but that is it! This is the "two text rule." Most of the time if a girl doesn't get back to me I won't even send a second text, but sometimes the situation calls for it. One example is the other day I texted a girl in the morning and did not get a response. However, later that evening I sent her another text, totally unrelated to the first, and she got back to me. Sometimes it works, sometimes it doesn't. Just don't send more than two.

Spelling and Grammar

This only occurs with certain gentleman, however you may be one of them. You texts should not look like you haven't passed 3rd grade. You really should try and put some effort into your text messages. Spell out words, put periods and question marks at the end of sentences, make your texts readable! You don't want girls to misread your text and get mad or even worse, not be able to understand your message!

Now I'm not saying you need to text like a college English professor, but do not text girls like you were raised on the streets of Compton. Here's an example of a *bad* text:

"Ay grl, wht u up 2 tonite"

A better text would look like:

"Hey Sarah! What are you up to tonight?"

I hope you see the difference and who this girl would want to go on a date with.

Message Length

Another good rule of thumb to remember when texting girls is to try to respond to her messages with messages of equal length. This isn't always doable, like when she is giving you one word responses, but try to do it when you can. If a girl is hitting you with short messages, send her short ones back. If she's writing long messages with good content, emoticons, and seems really interested, you can return the favor.

Understand that most girls won't text you if they truly don't want to talk to you at all. So if she is texting you one word answers or her texts seem dull, she may just be having a bad day or be busy. Stop texting her and try again another day.

Emoticons

The next thing I want to go over is emoticons. When I first started texting I thought using smiley faces and other emoticons was rather feminine, but I soon realized that there is not much emotion that can be displayed via text messages and girls can easily misinterpret your messages if you're not careful. So after a little bit I decided emoticons are okay and should be used in certain situations. One situation in which you'd use an emoticon is if your texting a girl something and it could be taken the wrong way. Just add a ":P" at the end, and it immediately becomes a playful joke. With that being said, emoticons should be used *sparingly*. I still find them kind of feminine, but like I said, they are needed in certain situations. So after certain jokes, or in the last text of the night, go ahead and put in that smiley face, but don't overdo it! You do not want to be known as the smiley face guy. I've seen some guys that use smiley faces or tongue out faces in every text message they send and it just gets annoying and weird from a girls perspective. Not only does the emoticon lose its meaning, but it makes you look nervous and insecure. So use emoticons sparingly!

Other items you can use to add emotion to your texts are exclamation marks and question marks. Exclamation marks make the text exciting! It makes you seem happy and gives the text conversation more energy! Just look at these two text messages and compare the difference:

1. *hey jessica hope your week went well feel like mines never going to end.*

2. *Hey Jessica! Hope your week went well :) Feel like mines never going to end!*

As you can easily tell, there is much more energy and emotion in texts when using emoticons and exclamation points. This makes your messages look more fun, vivid, and engaging. Unlike real conversations, when texting you do not have body language, tone of voice, or other indicators to judge how someone feels. So these little tools are really all you have to liven up messages. And even though using too many emoticons may be viewed as "feminine," they have more upsides than downsides for sparking the right emotions and building attraction over texts with women.

Now let's go over "haha" and "lol". This is another common thing, just like the emoticons, that some guys over-do in their text messages. Putting "haha" or "lol" at the end of everything you send a girl makes it look like you are laughing at your own joke and makes you look nervous. For example:

- *"hey whats up. Lol"*
- *"you end up seeing that movie? Lol*
- *"why'd you go there haha"*

You seem nervous and unsure of yourself when you end all your texts with "haha" or "lol". I see this way too often and it's a problem some guys have. You can use "lol" or "haha" at the end of texts, but just like emoticons use these softeners sparingly and only when the message calls for it. And when you do use them, a good rule is instead of putting them at the end of the text, put them at the beginning.

- *"lol you end up seeing that movie?"*
- *"haha why'd you go there?"*

This sets up the joke and doesn't make you look so nervous, laughing at your own statement. We all know the guy or girl in real life who laughs after everything they say... don't be that person.

Girl Lingo

The next thing you need to understand is what certain responses from girls mean and how to handle them. If you're texting a girl and she sends one or two worded responses like "okay" or "oh cool", she's either not in the mood to be texting or not really into you. You need to understand this and re-think how to approach her. If you keep texting her when she's giving you obvious signals she doesn't want to text, this will only push her further away from you and lessen any chance you have with her. In this situation, stop texting her, go back to the drawing board, and try again another day.

Most of the time, being a guy, you have to be the one who initiates contact with a girl. Some girls are more outgoing and will text you first. No matter the case though, if a girl texts you first, she is most likely interested in you. For a girl to text a guy takes some guts on her part and she didn't just text you out of the blue to get to know your opinion on politics or what you think of a TV show. Ninety nine times out of a hundred if a girl texts you first, she is into you. Use this to your advantage.

Another sign that a girl is into you is if she is using emoticons in her texts. Many times girls will use emoticons as a signal that they're flirting with you. An example would be if you've texted her to meet somewhere and she responds with, "Okay. See you later :)". She didn't have to put a smiley face at the end, however she didn't put it there for no reason; that smiley face is a sly signal from her that she is into you and happy you are texting her.

Now I want to bring up something that guys do WAY too often… and it has to do with texting. Texting is **NOT** the time to have full on conversations asking any question you can possibly think of to keep the conversation going. The main purpose of texting is simply to make her smile and laugh, flirt with her, keep her thinking about you, get her on the phone, then get her on a date.

To recap, being creative, interesting, humorous, fun, a challenge, and unpredictable is the key to being a better texter and achieving the results you want with girls. You also want to text sparingly and remember texting should be used as a tool to advance with a girl to the phone or on a date; it should not be the only tool you use when talking to girls.

When texting different girls you have to keep something in mind... they're different. So some of the humor and pet names you use with one girl may completely backfire on you with others. What I'm saying is you can't use the exact same approach with every girl you text. My suggestion would be to feel a girl out and learn her personality before you send her something she could take the wrong way.

Oh, and I needed to include this in the book; when doing research I talked to a lot of girls and you know what they can't stand... opening up their phone to a picture of your dick! I don't know what ass hole started this but **STOP** sending pictures of your dick to girls. Girls are not like guys and do not get horny seeing a guy's junk on their phone. It makes you look like a weirdo **AND** if you ever piss this girl off she now has a picture of your dick which she can print out and place anywhere she wants! I knew a girl who made a guy dress his dick up as a president every time he wanted to send her a picture. Why did she do this? So she could laugh at him and show all her friends. So what's the moral of this story... do not send dick pics... please stop guys.

Timing

Many guys (with my previous self included), think after you get a girl's number, you should immediately start texting her, and then start texting her every day after that. You should add her on Snapchat, and Facebook and Instagram. This is so she will remember you, like you, bond with you, etc. Then you should keep the text conversations with her going all the time, and ask her on date as soon as you can.

THIS IS ALL WRONG

From everything I've told you in this book, you know this is wrong and you may be guilty of this yourself; I know I was. You do not want to do any of this, as I have previously explained. If you're going to add her on social media, start with just one platform. If you do add her on more, wait a couple weeks before you do it. I've heard of guys adding girls on all platforms at the same time as soon as they meet them. HUGE TURN OFF. Complete opposite of challenge.

You really want to be texting this girl a max of 2 times a week. I usually get a girl's number, text her the next day, and then don't text her again for 3 days. This goes back to unpredictability and challenge. You do not want to be always available, always there, always in touch with her. You want her to miss you. You want her to think about you. How do you do this? You don't text her every day.

Another thing that relates to timing is who leaves first. You always want to be the first one to go. Whether that be by actually saying "got to go, ttyl", or if you just stop texting her back. What this does is make her miss you. She also will start to analyze her text and think to herself:

- *Why isn't he texting me back?*
- *Did I say something wrong?*
- *Does he like me?*

It puts you in control of the conversation. Many times too, when you start doing this, the girl will end up texting you the next day, or later on in the week. This is because she starts to miss you.

Persistence

For many girls, persistence will be a big factor when it comes to getting her on a date versus playing the one man trombone in your room. There is however a fine line between being persistent and being a clinger. You are NOT being a clinger here. Being persistent does not mean sneaking into her window late at night because she didn't text you back that day, or calling her 24 times in 24 hours. What is meant by "persistence" is sticking to the rules laid out in this book in regards to timing, being a challenge, etc. but not giving up after the first time she doesn't text you back. Even when she is sometimes giving you those one word answers or maybe doesn't text you back for a few hours, it's okay. Stop texting her and try again another time but don't let her go. Let me give you an example.

I met a girl on Tinder recently and had been texting her on and off for a few months. I asked her on a date via text and she told me she was busy and couldn't do anything without giving me a raincheck. Now usually this means a girl isn't into you, however as I said before, if she is still texting you back and responding to your messages, she most likely still has some interest in you. While I was ready to throw in the towel and flush her number down the toilet, I waited a week and started texting her again. After a little bit, I again asked her on a date and she agreed. We met at an ice cream shop, and things went well. Had I given up and not been persistent, I would have never gotten a date with this girl. So if you really like a girl, don't give up; be persistent!

Chapter 5
Initiating Contact

Okay so you got her number and are ready to contact her. First off, do **NOT** do that stupid three day rule. I don't know who made that up, but you just met this girl and she barely knows you. You want those emotions and sparks that were just flying to be with her when she gets that first text from you. If you wait three days or longer to text her she will most likely have a hard time remembering the whole interaction you two had, may forget certain things, and the emotions she felt for you will have dwindled down more and more with each day that's gone by. So I would suggest contacting her later that day, or the next day, but no later than that. And considering the girls in this day and age, text her first, do **NOT** call her yet.

Here is one approach you can take when first contacting a girl, text her something like this:

"Hey it's Zac from [however you met her]. Here's my number."

Then, no matter what she sends you, don't respond that day. What this waiting does is totally throws her off. She won't know what think. Girls want what they can't have.

Make sure the first time you text a girl you do not bring up her looks. The more attractive this girl is, the more likely every other guy has told her how beautiful she is. You want to stand out and be different. She needs to earn that comment on her looks once she gets to know you better. You can bring up her personality, cool things she may be interested in, etc., but don't bring up physical appearance in the beginning. You will seem different from other guys.

Another point I want to touch on is make sure you do not text girls how interested you are in them. Once you tell a girl "you want her," all mystery and sexual tension is gone. She can think you want her, guess you want her, but she cannot KNOW you want her until you are in a solid relationship with her. Girls want what they can't have, and when you give away all your feelings via text, all the mystery is dead and she will be less interested now because she knows you are hers; remember this. You always want her to be on the fence, wondering if you are actually into her. It will keep her very interested in you.

I will usually initiate contact with a girl the day after I meet her. I open up with a fun opener, send a few texts back and forth, am the first to leave, and then don't text her again for another 3 days.

Chapter 6
Texting

This is going to be the big chapter because this is the heart of this book, texting, so let's get started!

I noticed when I first started texting girls I was putting them on a pedestal and over-analyzing my text messages, and it led to bad results. You got to text her with the mentality that you're just being yourself and don't care what she thinks. I know, easier said than done, but when you over-analyze your text messages and put her on a pedestal, you end up sending her stupid texts, look nervous, and don't appear confident. Switch it around and think of yourself as the prize, not her. You will feel more confident and it will show in your texts.

Openers

Okay so now you have a better understanding of text messages, what they're used for, and the women who will be receiving them. Now I'm going to start going over opening lines. Do any of these text messages look familiar?

- *Hey whats up*

- *Hey beautiful*

- *Hey what you doing*

- *Whats good*

- *How was your day*

Now once in a while a message like "hey what you doing" is okay, but you don't want this to be the only thing you ever send girls. Some better opening messages would be:

- "You getting into any trouble tonight?"

- "Hey Jessica! What you doing?"

- "Stop creeping my facebook."

- "I saw someone outside hiding in my bushes last night. Just be honest... was it you?"

- "Hey there (nickname)."

- A question about current events, celebrities, or something else she can relate to.

- "Aliens are coming tomorrow to take all the sexy people… I just wanted to text you to say bye"

- "All we ever do is have text. I feel like our relationship could use some calls too"

- A cheezy pick up line like:

  You: *Jeez I'm tired*
  Her: *Why is that?*
  You: *Running around your dreams all night!*

- "It's 11:11! Make a wish."

- "Just wanted you to feel me vibrate"

- "If Italy invaded France from the rear, would Greece help?"

- "Just making sure you haven't stopped thinking about me."

- "Beautiful eyes, an incredible body, a big brain, a sexy mouth, a nice smile…but enough about me, tell me a little about you."

- "Stop thinking about me!"

- "I've given it some thought and I think we should just be friends with sexual tension."

- "You wouldn't believe the dream I had last night!"

- "It's me, your cell phone, not wanting anything in particular right now, just wanted to get out of your pocket. The smell is unbearable, take care."

- "Maybe it's the booze talking, but I want you to know I love booze."

- "Did I just see you??"

- "Knock knock.."

- "Out of all the (first name) (last name)'s I know... I think you're my favorite."

- "Stop making me think about you. I have stuff to do today"

- "Funniest thing... was just in Saks and bumped into your friend. Interesting :)"

- "That's it, I want a divorce. What are we going to do with the f'in cat?"

- "I just saw something that reminded me of you"

- "I'm in the mall, trying on cologne. Which smells better, the one on my right wrist, or the one on my left?"

- Me and my friend keep arguing and I need to settle the debate. Are khakis a color or a fabric?

- "**You:** *Hey can you keep a secret?*

Her: Sure, what's up?

You: I met this girl who is really nice, but I think all she wants to do is get in my pants.

- "If you were my coworker, I'd sexually harass you"

- I wish you were on Facebook because I would poke you.

- *You: 3x + 5y = 8*9y (solve for x, then graph y)*

  Her: Huh?

  You: you make me harder than an algebra problem

With these texts you are trying to pique her curiosity because let's be honest, women just **HAVE** to know stuff.

When talking to girls, it's a good idea to say their name. "Hey Jessica! What you doing?" Psychology teaches us that people love hearing their own name. Do this when texting, e-mailing, and talking on the phone as it makes the conversation seem more personal; I highly recommend it.

Hooks

Now I want to talk about something called "hooks." When a girl responds to your text messages, she will include things in her texts called "hooks." Hooks are important words or phrases which give you ammunition you can use to further the conversation. The real magic in hooks is you don't need to capitalize on them right away and shouldn't always right away, as you can save them to use later on in the texting conversation. So if a conversation gets boring or you can't think of anything to say, just bring up a previous hook to keep things alive. You can also put hooks in your own texts so she is more likely to ask you questions and keep the conversation going. I'm going to show an example conversation and underline the hook points:

Zac: Hey there :P

Girl: What's up :P
> (Notice she is putting the burden on me to carry the conversation)

Zac: I'm just <u>watching an awesome movie</u>... and texting you. What are you up to?
> (I'm giving her a hook here to use. Notice I did not tell her the name of the movie on purpose, so she will be curious and ask me questions.)

Girl: <u>I love movies</u>! <u>What movie is it</u>?

(There are actually two hooks here. The first one where she says "I love movies" is kind of subtle, but from it, we can derive conversations about how she should come over my place and watch a movie sometime. The second hook is more obvious as you can explain to her the movie you're watching.)

Zac: So do I! It's called "how high," have you ever seen it?

(I ask her a question here so she will continue responding and we can keep this conversation going.)

Now let's look at a conversation where she gives you hooks to talk about:

Zac: Hola amiga

Girl: Hey Zac!

Zac: I'm at work about to punch my computer screen! What are you doing?

Girl: I'm out with my friends a <u>bar called Portofinos</u>.

Zac: Portofinos? Have you tried the long island iced tea there?

Girl: No I haven't. Is it good?

Zac: Oh it's amazing. Is that your favorite bar?

Girl: Yeah, I love this place!

Zac: Yeah it's awesome. I'll let you go, have fun with your friends, see ya!

This is a pretty typical text conversation for me. It may go a little longer, but I keep it pretty simple. I text her something fun as the opener, talk with her a little, use a hook to elaborate the conversation, and then leave, making her want more. Then I'll maybe text her again in 2-3 days to do it again, and eventually ask her to talk on the phone or go on a date. Notice I am not going on long winded, boring text conversations that go nowhere.

I also underlined the hook she gave me, the bar Portofinos, which I could talk with her about.

Something else I picked up on a forum, that is a good idea, is to give *her* a hook in your opening message. Look in my text above; she did not even ask me what I was doing, however I started the text with "at work, about the punch the computer screen". This gives her a hook to ask you "why are you doing that lol". It can create a nice text conversation.

So now you know what "hooks" are. The thing about hooks is plenty of them will come up when you're texting a girl and they make it easy to keep the text conversation alive. And like I said, you can always come back to a hook or bring up a hook from days ago such as how she loves movies and you two should watch a movie together in the future. Notice in this conversation though I did not bring up anything about going on a date, coming over, etc. because I'm just starting to get to know this girl. You want to gain her interest over text, and make sure enough rapport is built before you bring up going out somewhere with her. You have a much better chance of getting her to say yes to a date when she feels comfortable with you.

Questions

It's good to use questions when texting a girl. Notice in the example conversation above, I asked the girl questions in my text. I really try to put questions in a lot of my texts. With questions, you know you should get a response to your text; there is no in-between thinking. With a statement, she's not really obligated to respond, she might not respond, then you don't know what she is thinking… it can create issues. Then you're forced to text her again because you haven't gotten a response and it could have just been because she was just busy. With questions, you can just wait. There is no need for a second text. If she doesn't respond, she either isn't into you, or is busy and you just need to wait.

Now obviously you don't want to start interrogating a girl, making every message a question. It's just a good rule to remember when texting to include questions. Make sure to end your question with a "?" as well, as sometimes girls just glance at their phone and she will be more likely to realize you texted her a question.

What if She Isn't Responding?

If for some reason a girl doesn't respond to your text, give it time. It could be you, but it might not be. People are sometimes busy, people have bad days, and a variety of other things could be going on. I wasn't getting a response from a girl the other day and thought "great, what the heck happened." Well it turns out her phone got stolen at the mall and she didn't get a new one for three days! So if a girl doesn't answer your text, don't freak out. Don't start texting her a bunch of times in a row hoping to get a response, you will look desperate. Instead just give it some time. Stick to the "no response" rules I brought up in chapter 4. While you're waiting to text her go over the texts you sent, rethink your strategy, and see if you could have done anything differently.

It isn't always possible to turn things around when a girl doesn't text you back... but sometimes it is. The best thing I've noticed is time. Here's the rules I usually go by if a girl doesn't respond:

- She doesn't reply once: give her a week of text silence.
- She doesn't reply twice: give her a month of text silence.

- She doesn't reply three times: flush her number down the toilet.

When a girl doesn't text back or when a girl doesn't call back, the first thing to remember is *don't panic*! It's not the end of the world, and it doesn't mean you've lost her for good.

Make sure you do not send follow-up texts after being ignored. Think about this, she hasn't texted you back at all but you've texted her three times; what does this say about you? It definitely doesn't make you appear confident and it makes you look needy; a turn off for women. It also shows a clear signal that you are into her, making any mystery about you vanish.

I have a last ditch effort trick that I use when it seems all is lost, and a girl has stopped responding to my texts or is giving me all one word answers. This does not work all the time, but it can. And what do you have to lose if she hasn't been responding right?

Stop texting her for a few days and then send her this:

"olive garden it is! I'll pick you up at 7pm :)"

Then when she responds say:

"oh sorry, wrong number"

…and stop texting her. This will make her mad, she'll think you're a jerk, but she **WILL** start thinking about you, and she will definitely get jealous. It's a good trick to re-connect with a girl who is being a brat. Then wait about a week and try texting her again as if nothing happened.

Ignoring Texts

While I'm on the topic of girls ignoring your texts, remember it is perfectly acceptable for you to ignore her texts too! Actually I encourage you to not respond to all of her texts and not to always initiate conversation. Think about how much it gets to you when you text a girl and she blatantly ignores it and doesn't send you a response… well it does the same thing to her! So not all the time, but occasionally you should just stop responding, respond at a much later time, or completely ignore her text; this goes back to the "challenge" factor.

If you have an iPhone, you know about iMessenger. Within your text, you can leave a "read" receipt. Many people turn this option off because they do not want people to see when they've read their texts. I actually encourage you to turn it on. How much does it eat you up inside when someone leaves you on read, and does not text you back? You know they read it, but they aren't responding! Well, you can now do this to girls. When she texts you and you read it, she will see that. Then when you haven't responded in 1 hour, 2 hours, or maybe don't even respond at all, it will start to get to her. This goes back to "girls want what they can't have."

Text Rapport

When a girl texts you, you can use her response to tell a story that somehow relates to what she says. Some of the most powerful examples involve stories which show how you felt the same way as she did. What these stories do is make her feel more comfortable with you and make her feel like she can relate to you. She's basically giving you a hook, and you are just using it to relate to her. Let me give you an example:

> *Girl: I just started my new job today, it's kind of scary.*
>
> *Zac: I totally know what you mean. When I started my last job, I was so nervous my first day that I managed to trip and spill my boss's coffee all over him!*
>
> *Girl: Really??*
>
> *Zac: I hope your first day doesn't go that bad :P*

You just told a little story about yourself showing that you two have some things in common. You also are allowing her to talk about her day and get a conversation going. These short stories you make up don't have to actually have happened. You can make it up or stretch the truth a little. Building comfort via relating is key to longer, better conversation and building attraction.

Why?

Never ask the "why" question. When you ask a girl "why" she isn't texting you, you are putting everything out on the table. You're displaying clear signs of interest, that you care about her, and you want her to text you! All the mystery surrounding you is abolished. In girl world, this can have dire consequences, so no matter how much you may be thinking it, do **not** ask a girl why she isn't texting you.

If she doesn't care enough to text you back, you have to not care why, or at least act like you don't care and it doesn't bother you. This will make you look much more confident then asking a girl, especially one you don't know that well, why she isn't texting you back.

You just have to look at the situation, rethink your strategy, and think about what you could have done better. And even if you did ask her "why," she's never going to tell you the truth. She would most likely say something like "been busy" or "didn't have my phone", but she would be lying. That's the reason asking "why" is just silly to do.

Sorry

This is very similar to what I just brought up with "why." You should never say "sorry" when you text a girl. You may be tempted to say this if you think you texted a girl something that could be taken the wrong way, and she hasn't responded for a few days, and you just think apologizing will fix the issue... it won't. Saying sorry over text is one of the worst things you can do, next to asking why. It does the same thing and shows that you like her, she is in control, and you're a wuss. All things that negate any mystery or challenge you may have displayed.

If you actually think you f'd up and texted her something she took offense to, the best factor on your side is time. I would say wait a week, and then try texting her again. Do not even bring up whatever you texted her, just start on a new topic. Talk about something in the news, or celebrity gossip. With time, what you said may not be a big deal to her anymore, or she may have even forgotten about it.

Out of Context

When you're texting girls, and you have built some rapport with her (don't use this on brand new girls), take things out of context as if you secretly know she is just hitting on you.

Her: *I'm going to bed, good night.*

You: Wow! I don't know you that well. I'm sleeping in my own bed tonight, nice try though.

Here's another example:

Her: Have you seen that new movie The Hunger Games?

You: Are you inviting me on a date? That's really nice, but I'll only go if you buy me popcorn and a soda. No exceptions.

What this "out of context" strategy does is makes her laugh and builds sexual tension. You also can use ambiguity and double entendre to slip lines in texts which could, but don't have to be, taken in a sexual way.

Time

When you're texting girls, it's cool to mix up the times you text her; sometimes send her a text before she wakes up, sometimes a text at night. Try to be random, and don't text her all day. When you text girls all day and every day, you're not helping yourself. The first reason for this is because you'll probably start to annoy her texting her so much. The second reason for this is because you begin to lose all the mystery and attraction she may have perceived in you because you are constantly sharing everything with her. You got to turn it around sometimes and think about things from a girl's perspective. What would it be like if some girl you knew texted you every day, all day, with silly things you don't really care about? It would get annoying! So you should try to mix up your texts and be unpredictable; sometimes let a day go by, sometimes a week go by, sometimes in the morning, sometimes at night. Mix it up and make her wonder when you are going to be texting her. And then if the conversation is going well, you can continue texting her, but don't grab for straws if there isn't much to say. You build attraction and comfort with a girl on the date, so the focus of your text messages should be to get to that.

Nicknames

Nicknames are great inside jokes that you and a girl can use with each other. It's something playful that she will remember and will make her smile. The best way of coming up with a nickname is to connect it to something specific about her; maybe something related to her personality, or one of her favorite activities, or ever about her looks.

Here are some examples for nicknames you could use:

- Sugar

- Honey
- Buttercup
- Cupcake
- Firefox
- Snorkle Bum
- Tongue Slider
- Sassy-Pants
- Nerdball
- Sex Panther
- Tiger Baby
- Speed Racer
- Little Brat
- Turtle Dove
- Sweet Face
- Cheeseball
- Chatty Cat
- Baby Seal
- Dirty Girl
- Pixie Dust
- Cranky Puss
- Moaning Lisa
- Love Bomb
- Ditzoid
- Cyber Slave

- Goofy Loo
- Stupid Head
- Lint Licker
- Grabby Hands

Don't be afraid of using these little special nicknames when you're messaging girls; actually I highly suggest it! It adds so much fun to text conversations.

Future Projection

Future projection is a texting technique where you talk about things that you and a girl will do together in the future. It's a nice subtle technique because it's not a direct date, it is just a vaguely implied date that might happen. This makes it "safe" for a woman to agree to it. It subconsciously conditions her to agree to a real date in the future. It also provides you with a hook you can use to text her in the future. Here's an example of using future projection:

Girl: Oh yes it's raining, I love the rain!

Zac: Oh no way, me too! Okay next time it rains we're going to walk around in it!

Girl: lol okay

Zac: I hope you don't get mad when I throw you in a puddle :P

Notice how the future projection isn't a huge thing, it's just small, fun, and light. It's non-committing and just fun and flirty. There is also some implied touching and sexuality when I joked about throwing her in the puddle. You and this girl may never actually walk in the rain in the future, but it now becomes a possibility. And then the next time it rains you have something to text her about. Future projection can be a very powerful tool for creating attraction.

Ending Conversations

You should always try to be the first one who says bye or gtg. This makes you look busy (which means you are doing stuff in life) and will leave her wanting more because you aren't texting her anymore. Think about when you're texting a girl and all of a sudden she says something like, "ttyl, I'm going to a concert". You start thinking about her, wonder why she didn't invite you to the concert, etc. Well you can do the same to her! It's good to say you "gtg" because you are doing stuff with friends, going to a party, going to get dinner, etc. These are examples showing you have a great social life and people like you. Girls want to be around guys who people like. It's called "social proof." So always be the first one who ends the conversation; this is a very big deal.

Multiple Girls

Another good technique is to not just text one girl but to text multiple girls at the same time. You do not want to put all your eggs in one basket, because the one girl you are texting may not work out, and then what? Not only that, when you are texting multiple girls, you will not worry so much if one girl doesn't text you back. It really helps so you don't obsess so much over one girl as there are now many you are talking to. So send a girl a text, then move on to the next girl and forget about the first text. You end up looking extremely attractive to all these girls because you end up implementing some tips I brought up before such as not always texting back, saying you gtg, making her wait for a text, etc. This is because you are ACTUALLY busy talking to multiple girls.

Moving to the Phone

Now the phone may not be a move you make with every girl, but for some, you may decide you two are really clicking, and you want to talk to her over the phone or on Facetime. In order to do this, a good idea is to set up the phone call with a text message. When you set up a phone call with a text message, girls are much more likely to answer versus a cold call out of nowhere. Here are a few examples of how you could set up a phone call:

"Oh, I'm getting kind of busy right now, I'll call you later"

(Use this after texting back and forth a few times.)

"Oh what, I got to hear more about this, I'm going to call you."

(Use this when you're texting each other juicy gossip or some interesting information.)

"Are you going to be free later around 8pm? Let's talk on the phone a little."

If you have a lot to say, call her! This is a prime opportunity to talk on the phone and instead of sending her a 10 page text message, you can build comfort with her on the phone.

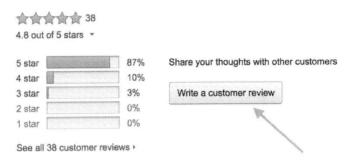

If you are enjoying this book, could you please leave a review on Amazon? It would be greatly appreciated and allow me to come out with more informative books in the future. A shortened link to the review page is below:

Linkpony.com/text

Chapter 7

Asking Her on a Date

I've noticed when asking girls on dates that I'm the most successful when I have built comfort and rapport with them. Once you ask a girl out and she says "no," it's much harder to get a yes in the future. So I would suggest waiting till you have built comfort and rapport with a girl before you even bring up hanging out with her.

Something you never want to do is ask a girl on a date as soon as you meet her, or within the first few texts you send her. If you use dating apps like Tinder, it's the same principles. Don't ask her on a date over Tinder. Wait until you interacted with her a little while and have built rapport.

There are two ways to ask a girl on a date: via a text message or over the phone. This is going to have to be your choice. I'd say doing it over the phone is slightly more advantageous, just because there is more of a personal feel to it. However some girls don't like talking on the phone at all, and you can only reach them through text. If this is the case, you'll have to go via text. But if you do sometimes talk to her via Facetime or over the phone, go that route. A way to do this would be to call her and ask her on a date. Don't talk about life, the president, etc. Just ask her on a date and hang up. Make this a quick call. In sales I learned the phone is for making appointments, not for selling the client. As in you'll build attraction on the date, not on the phone call.

Whether you choose to text or call her, you want to have everything planned. Don't call her and say "hey wanna go out sometime... idk where do you want to go?" As a guy, we are expected to lead and take control; girls find this attractive. As such, you want to have a plan made when you call or text her for a date. Ask her if she's free on a certain day that is at least 2 days out from when you are talking to her. Then when you both agree on a day, YOU need to suggest both a time and place for you to meet her; do not ask her where she wants to go. This is a common mistake guys commit, making them appear insecure. If she doesn't like your suggestion she will tell you and suggest something else. You need to lead and take control of situations; girls like that.

So you've been texting a girl for a little while, you've talked to her on the phone, you've built up some comfort with her, and you're ready to ask her on a date. Let's say it's Wednesday night and you haven't texted her in a few days. Here is an example of a good text to send her:

You: *"Hey are you free Saturday night? We should go get some coffee at Starbucks."*

Her: *"Yeah, that sounds good"*

You: *"Awesome. Let's plan for 7:01pm. What's your address?*

Her: *123 Easy St, Dixie, NH 12345*

You: *Got it, see ya then!*

If a girl is into you she'll most likely agree to the date. If she is into you and for some reason is busy and can't go, she'll most likely ask you if there is another day you can go or give you an alternate time to meet. If a girl just straight up says, "no, can't go" without an explanation or rain check, then there was no line that was going to get her on a date with you. This means she isn't into you.

I brought up coffee in this example because it's a great first date. You can chat with the girl, be close to her, it's cheap, and you're in a nice public environment where you both feel comfortable. When you ask for the date, ask if you can pick her up. Sometimes girls are okay with this, even on the first date. This just adds a little time to your date, and makes it easier to move in for a kiss at the end of the date when you drop her off at her house.

When going out with a girl, pay for the date. In the past I used to split the check, but I've had girls stop talking to me over this. Girls like it when a guy pays for the first date, especially in certain parts of the country like the south.

Sometimes you may get a girl out on a date and then realize you want absolutely nothing to do with her! She may look nothing like her photos, or have a horrendous personality. Here is another reason why a quick coffee date is so valuable. You only paid like $2 for her drink, you took an hour of your life, and things are done. You can say thanks, drop her off, and go home. Imagine taking a girl, who after the first 5 minutes you find repulsive, to a $50 dinner. You're out hours of your life and $50!

And let's say you do like her, and the coffee date is going well; you can extend the date, and bond a little closer with the girl you're with. You can go to a park and look at the stars, go to an arcade, etc. An extended date like this also gives you a much better chance for the first kiss.

I really like the coffee date, and I don't really stray from it. If it isn't for you though, here are some more examples of first date ideas:

- Bowling
- Hiking
- Aquarium

- Pet Smart or Petco (It's a free zoo!)
- Actual theatre with actors on stage
- Driving range
- Art gallery or museum
- Local live band
- Play tourist in your own town, or a city near you
- Ice skating
- Try a new restaurant

Something that is unique I like to do when setting up dates is to use "odd times." So instead of telling her to meet you at Starbucks at 7:00 or 7:30, tell her 7:12 or 8:03. The reason this works is because it's silly and stands out! She notices it, laughs, and will remember you by it. I mean seriously, who tells a girl to meet him at 7:03… you do!

Now I don't go into much detail on what to do during the date or afterwards because this book is focused on texting. In my new book *How to Attract Women* (linkpony.com/women) I do go over this, as well as much more in regards to attracting females and the female psyche. The link above will bring you to that book. I highly recommend you check it out!

Let's just say that the date went well, you dropped off your date at her house, and are back at home after the date. If a girl texts you after the date saying how she had a good time, she had fun, etc. she is into you and wants to go out again! If a girl is into a guy, she will almost always text him after the date, or at least by the next day, but usually within that same night. If a girl does not text you after the date, it most likely means she does not like you. I would suggest waiting a week and then try texting her. She may have a change of heart by then, and it also establishes some challenge on your part.

Conclusion

Well I hoped you enjoyed the book and learned a great deal of information from it. Texting is always evolving and changing, but with these tips you should have a much better handle on texting girls and a better understanding of the general rules of texting.

I have more books and articles on my website at **GetMoreDates.com**, as well as a VIP Coaching section where you can get personal advice from me to help you attract women. Be sure to check it out for more help. I wish you well in your pursuit of women and good luck with texting!

If you liked this book, you may also enjoy:

How to Attract Women

The Last of the Dating Books You'll Ever Need to Get the Girls You've Always Wanted

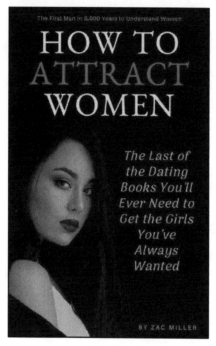

Link to Amazon Page:
linkpony.com/women

Girls have been a mystery for thousands of years however one man has finally figured them out. In *How to Attract Women*, author Zac Miller goes over the entire process of attracting women. Appearance, conversation topics, psychological techniques, body language, and much more… it's all included in this book! **You can** be with the girl of your dreams! Find out how now in *How to Attract Women*.

MATCHED

How to Get Girls on Tinder, Bumble, or Any Other
Dating App or Website

Link to Amazon Page:
linkpony.com/match

Struggling when it comes to getting girls on dating apps like Tinder & Bumble? Zac Miller has you covered! In his new book MATCHED, he goes over everything when it comes to getting girls on dating apps. The bio, the pictures, the messages, and the date - it's all covered! Find out more at the link above!

The Crash Signal

The One Signal That Predicts a Stock Market Crash

Link to Amazon Page:
linkpony.com/crash

If you know anything about the stock market, you know crashes are inevitable... but losing money in those crashing doesn't have to be! In this book, Tim Morris shows you the one signal which has flashed before every stock market crash for the last 60 years! Will you be prepared for the next crash? Save your money before it's too late with The Crash Signal!

Made in United States
Orlando, FL
18 September 2023